I0012142

Table of Contents

Introduction: A Warm Welcome to the World of Podcasting

Welcome to "The Ultimate Guide on How to Start a Podcast." I'm so glad you're here. In our fast-paced digital world, podcasts have taken off in a big way. They've become an incredibly popular and powerful medium for communication and storytelling. Whether you're a budding entrepreneur or a seasoned business owner, starting a podcast could be a real game-changer for your personal brand and business growth.

This book is here to provide you with a detailed roadmap on how to launch your very own podcast from scratch. Trust me, by the end of this journey, you'll have all the tools and knowledge you need to get your podcast up and running.

So, what can you expect from the chapters ahead? We're going to dive deep into every essential aspect of podcasting. We'll cover everything from the initial planning stages, through to recording, editing, and publishing your episodes. But that's not all – we'll also explore how to promote your podcast, engage with your audience, and even monetize and grow your podcast over time.

Throughout this guide, I'll be with you every step of the way, offering tips, advice, and insights to help you navigate the exciting world of podcasting. So, let's get started and turn your podcasting dreams into reality!

Chapter 1: Introduction to Podcasting

Welcome to the exciting world of podcasting! In this chapter, we're going to dive into the fascinating rise of podcasting as a popular medium. We'll chat about how podcasts have captured the hearts and ears of listeners all around the globe and unpack the reasons behind their booming success.

Let's start by exploring why podcasts have become such a hit. Imagine being able to listen to engaging, informative, and entertaining content while you're on the go – whether you're commuting, working out, cooking, or just relaxing at home. This flexibility and convenience are huge factors in why people love podcasts. They offer a unique blend of storytelling, expert insights, and personal connections that traditional media often can't match.

Podcasts have also tapped into the modern need for multitasking. In today's fast-paced world, finding time to sit down and read a book or watch a lengthy video can be challenging. But with podcasts, you can easily integrate learning and entertainment into your daily routine. This on-the-go accessibility has significantly contributed to their popularity.

Now, let's talk about why you might want to start your own podcast. Whether you're an individual with a passion for a particular topic or a business looking to expand its reach, podcasting offers numerous benefits. One of the most compelling reasons is the opportunity to establish thought leadership. By sharing your knowledge and insights on a subject, you position yourself as an authority in your field. This can help you build credibility and trust with your audience.

Moreover, podcasting allows you to connect with your target audience in a more personal and intimate way. Unlike written content, podcasts let your listeners hear your voice, tone, and personality, creating a stronger bond and sense of connection. This can be incredibly powerful for building a loyal community around your brand or personal platform.

Starting a podcast also opens up opportunities for expanding your reach. Podcasts are easily shareable and can be distributed across various platforms, from Apple Podcasts and Spotify to social media and your own website. This wide distribution potential means you can reach a broader audience than through traditional blogging or video content alone.

By the end of this chapter, you'll grasp the importance of setting clear goals and objectives for your podcasting journey. Whether you aim to educate, entertain, inspire, or promote your business, having a defined purpose will guide your content creation and help you measure your success.

So, let's get ready to explore the wonderful world of podcasting together. By understanding its growth, benefits, and the importance of goal-setting, you'll be well-equipped to embark on your own podcasting adventure. Happy podcasting!

Chapter 2: Defining Your Podcast Concept

Welcome to Chapter 2! Now that we've got the basics covered, it's time to dive into something really exciting: defining your podcast concept. This is where your podcasting journey truly begins, and trust me, it's a lot of fun.

First things first, let's talk about finding your niche and identifying your target audience. Imagine you're throwing a party. If you invite everyone you know without considering their interests, the party might end up being a bit chaotic. But if you focus on inviting people who share a common interest—say, fans of mystery novels—the party will be a hit because everyone has something to talk about. The same principle applies to your podcast. By narrowing your focus to a specific subject or industry, you can position yourself as an expert in that area. Plus, you'll attract listeners who are genuinely interested in what you have to say. This makes for a much more engaged and loyal audience.

Now, you might be wondering how to choose your niche. Start by thinking about what you're passionate about. What topics can you talk about for hours without getting bored? What do you already know a lot about, or what are you eager to learn more about? This could be anything from cooking vegan meals to discussing the latest trends in tech. Once you have a few ideas, do a bit of research to see if there's an audience for those topics. Look at existing podcasts in those areas, check out social media groups, and read forums to get a sense of what people are talking about.

After you've pinpointed your niche, it's time to think about your target audience. Who are they? What are their interests and challenges? The more you understand your audience, the better you can tailor your content to meet their needs. For example, if you're starting a podcast about personal finance for young professionals, your target audience might be people in their 20s and 30s who are looking to manage their money better. Understanding their lifestyle, challenges, and preferences will help you create content that resonates with them.

Next up is brainstorming podcast topics and formats. This is where you get to be creative! Think about what kind of episodes you want to produce. Will you do interviews with experts in your field, or will you focus on storytelling and sharing personal experiences? Maybe you want to mix it up with a combination of solo episodes, guest interviews, and panel discussions. The key is to choose a format that not only aligns with your interests and expertise but also keeps your audience engaged.

And let's not forget about your unique value proposition. This is what sets your podcast apart from all the others out there. It's your special sauce. Ask yourself: Why should someone listen to my podcast instead of another one on the same topic? Maybe you have a unique perspective or a fresh approach to discussing your subject. Or perhaps you bring a level of expertise and insider knowledge that others don't. Whatever it is, make sure it's clear to your audience.

Finally, positioning your podcast effectively is crucial. This means figuring out how to market your podcast so that it reaches the right people. Think about your podcast's branding, including the name, logo, and overall aesthetic. Make sure it reflects the tone and content of your show. If your podcast is about something serious, like mental health, you might want a more subdued and professional look. If it's about something fun and light-hearted, like pop culture, you can go for a more vibrant and playful design.

In this chapter, we're going to walk you through each of these steps in detail. By the end, you'll have a clear, well-defined concept for your podcast that's ready to captivate and engage your audience. So grab a notebook, get comfortable, and let's get started on bringing your podcast vision to life!

Chapter 3: Planning Your Podcast Episodes

Welcome to Chapter 3, where we dive into the art of planning your podcast episodes. If you're looking to keep your listeners engaged and coming back for more, then you're in the right place. Let's talk about the essential steps to creating a podcast that's both well-organized and captivating.

First things first, let's introduce you to a crucial tool in your podcasting toolkit: the editorial calendar. Think of this as your roadmap to podcasting success. An editorial calendar is a schedule that outlines your podcast episodes over a set period, helping you maintain a consistent posting routine. Consistency is key in the podcasting world. Your listeners will appreciate knowing when to expect new content from you, and an editorial calendar ensures you can deliver just that.

Now, let's talk about structuring your episodes. This is where you can really capture your audience's attention and keep them hooked from start to finish. A well-structured episode is like a well-told story; it has a clear beginning, middle, and end. Start with an engaging introduction to grab your listeners' attention. Follow that with the main content, making sure to break it up into digestible segments. Finally, wrap things up with a strong conclusion that leaves your audience wanting more.

To help you stay on track and deliver a polished episode, it's a good idea to prepare show notes, outlines, and scripts. Show notes are brief summaries of your episodes that can guide your listeners through the content and provide additional resources or links. Outlines are your episode's skeleton, helping you organize your thoughts and flow of conversation. Scripts can be more detailed, providing a word-for-word guide if you prefer a more structured approach.

Using these tools not only keeps you organized but also ensures you cover all the important points without missing a beat. Plus, they can save you time during the editing process, making it easier to produce a smooth, professional-sounding final product.

In summary, Chapter 3 is all about planning your podcast episodes to create a seamless and engaging experience for your listeners. By using an editorial calendar, structuring your episodes effectively, and preparing thorough show notes, outlines, and scripts, you'll be well on your way to podcasting success. So, grab your planner, get organized, and let's start creating some fantastic episodes that your audience will love!

Chapter 4: Setting Up Your Podcast Equipment

Now that you've got a solid foundation for your podcast, it's time to dive into one of the most exciting parts: setting up your podcasting equipment. Trust me, having the right gear can make all the difference in producing high-quality audio content that your listeners will love.

In this chapter, we're going to take a closer look at the essential equipment you'll need to get started. We'll cover everything from microphones to headphones and recording software. Don't worry if you're feeling a bit overwhelmed by all the options out there; I'm here to help you navigate through it all.

Microphones

Let's start with microphones. This is arguably the most important piece of equipment you'll invest in. A good microphone will capture your voice clearly and reduce background noise, making your podcast sound professional. There are a few different types of microphones to consider:

1. Dynamic Microphones: These are great for beginners because they're durable and less sensitive to background noise.

They work well in less-than-ideal recording environments.

2. Condenser Microphones: These are more sensitive and capture a wider range of frequencies, resulting in richer sound quality. However, they can also pick up more background noise, so they work best in a controlled recording space.

Depending on your budget, you can find good-quality microphones in both categories. Some popular choices include the Audio-Technica ATR2100x-USB (dynamic) and the Audio-Technica AT2020 (condenser).

Headphones

Next up, let's talk about headphones. A good pair of headphones is essential for monitoring your recordings and editing your episodes. You'll want headphones that are comfortable for long periods and provide accurate sound reproduction. Over-ear, closed-back headphones are usually the best choice because they help isolate the sound and prevent audio bleed.

Some popular models to consider are the Sony MDR-7506 and the Audio-Technica ATH-M50x. Both are highly regarded in the podcasting and audio production communities.

Recording Software

Now that you've got your microphone and headphones sorted, you'll need some software to record and edit your episodes. There are several great options out there, ranging from free to professional-grade. Here are a few to consider:

1. Audacity: This is a free, open-source software that's perfect for beginners. It's easy to use and has all the basic features you need to get started.
2. GarageBand: If you're a Mac user, you probably already have this software installed. It's user-friendly and offers more advanced features as you become more comfortable with editing.
3. Adobe Audition: This is a professional-grade software with a lot of advanced features. It's perfect if you're looking to take your podcast production to the next level, but it does come with a subscription fee.

Setting Up Your Recording Space

Finally, let's talk about your recording space. Even the best equipment won't sound great if you're recording in a noisy or echoey environment. Here are some tips for setting up your recording space for optimal sound quality:

1. Choose a Quiet Room: Find a room in your home that's away from traffic noise and other potential disturbances. The quieter, the better.
2. Reduce Echo: Hard surfaces like walls and floors can cause sound to bounce around, creating an echo. You can reduce this by adding soft furnishings like rugs, curtains, and pillows. You can also hang blankets or foam panels on the walls to absorb sound.
3. Position Your Microphone Correctly: Make sure your microphone is positioned close to your mouth, but not so close that it picks up breathing sounds. Experiment with different angles and distances to find the best sound.

By the end of this chapter, you should have a clear understanding of the equipment you need and how to set up your recording space. Remember, producing high-quality audio content is key to creating a professional-sounding podcast that will keep your listeners coming back for more. So, take your time, do your research, and invest in the best equipment your budget allows. Happy podcasting!

Chapter 5: Recording and Editing Your Podcast

Welcome to Chapter 5! In this chapter, we're going to delve into the nuts and bolts of recording and editing your podcast. If you've ever wondered how to produce high-quality audio that captivates your audience and keeps them coming back for more, you're in the right place. So, let's get started!

First, let's talk about recording. The foundation of any great podcast is clear, crisp audio. You might have the most interesting content in the world, but if your listeners can't hear it properly because of background noise or poor sound quality, they'll quickly tune out. To help you avoid this, we've got some valuable tips to share.

One of the first things to consider is your recording environment. Ideally, you want to find a quiet space with minimal background noise. This could be a dedicated home studio, a quiet room, or even a closet filled with clothes to help absorb sound. If you're recording at home, let everyone know when you're recording to minimize interruptions. Also, consider turning off noisy appliances and closing windows to keep out external sounds.

Next up is your recording equipment. Investing

in a good quality microphone can make a world of difference. There are plenty of options out there, from USB microphones that plug directly into your computer to more advanced XLR microphones that require an audio interface. Choose one that fits your budget and needs. Additionally, using a pop filter can help reduce plosive sounds (like those pesky "p" and "b" sounds) that can distort your audio.

Once you've got your environment and equipment sorted, it's time to start recording. Pay attention to your microphone technique – keep a consistent distance from the mic and speak clearly. Don't worry if you make mistakes; you can always edit them out later. It's better to have multiple takes of a section than to settle for something you're not happy with.

Now, let's move on to the art of editing. Editing is where you can really polish your podcast episodes and make them shine. It's not just about cutting out mistakes; it's about improving the clarity, flow, and overall professionalism of your content.

One of the first steps in editing is to clean up your audio. This means removing any background noise, clicks, or other unwanted sounds. Most editing software, like Audacity or Adobe Audition, has tools to help with this. You'll also want to normalize your audio levels to ensure a consistent volume throughout the episode.

Next, focus on the flow of your episode. This might involve cutting out long pauses, filler words (like "um" and "uh"), or sections that don't add value to the conversation. Aim to keep your episodes engaging and to the point. Remember, your listeners' time is valuable, so make every minute count.

Adding intros, outros, music, and sound effects can significantly enhance your podcast and create a memorable experience for your listeners. An intro sets the tone for your episode and lets your audience know what to expect. It could be a brief musical piece, a voiceover, or a combination of both. Your outro is just as important, providing a sense of closure and a call to action for your listeners.

Music and sound effects can add an extra layer of professionalism and interest to your podcast. However, use them sparingly and ensure they complement rather than overpower your content. There are many royalty-free music libraries available where you can find the perfect tracks for your podcast.

By the end of this chapter, you'll have a solid understanding of how to record and edit your podcast to create high-quality, engaging episodes. With these skills in your toolkit, you'll be well on your way to producing a podcast that sounds great and keeps your audience coming back for more.

Happy recording and editing!

Chapter 6: Publishing Your Podcast

So, you've recorded your podcast episodes, edited them to perfection, and now you're ready to share them with the world. This is where the magic happens—publishing your podcast! In this chapter, we'll walk you through the entire process step by step, ensuring that your episodes reach as many listeners as possible.

First things first, let's talk about choosing a podcast hosting platform. Think of your hosting platform as your podcast's home base. This is where you'll store all your episodes and manage your podcast feed. There are plenty of hosting platforms out there, each with its own set of features and pricing plans. Some popular options include Libsyn, Podbean, Anchor, and Buzzsprout. Take some time to explore these platforms and see which one aligns best with your needs and budget.

Once you've selected a hosting platform, you'll need to set up your podcast's RSS feed. The RSS feed is essentially a file that contains all the information about your podcast—episode titles, descriptions, release dates, and so on. This feed is what podcast directories use to display your podcast to potential listeners. Don't worry if this sounds technical; most hosting platforms make it really easy to set up your RSS feed. They typically guide you through the process with simple, step-by-step instructions.

Next, let's dive into uploading and publishing your episodes. When you're ready to upload an episode, you'll need to fill out some details about it, such as the title, description, and any relevant tags or categories. These details are crucial because they help listeners find your podcast. Be sure to write clear, engaging titles and descriptions that accurately reflect the content of each episode. Once everything is filled out, you can hit the publish button, and voila—your episode is live!

But we're not stopping there. To reach the widest audience possible, you'll want to submit your podcast to popular directories like Apple Podcasts, Spotify, and Google Podcasts. Each of these platforms has its own submission process, but don't worry, we'll break it down for you.

Starting with Apple Podcasts, you'll need to create an Apple ID if you don't already have one. Then, log in to Apple Podcasts Connect and submit your podcast's RSS feed. Apple will review your submission, and once it's approved, your podcast will be available to millions of potential listeners.

For Spotify, the process is similar. Head over to Spotify for Podcasters, log in with your Spotify account, and submit your RSS feed. Spotify usually approves new podcasts quickly, so your episodes should be available on the platform in no time.

Google Podcasts also has a straightforward submission process. Go to the Google Podcasts Manager, sign in with your Google account, and submit your RSS feed. Google will then index your podcast, making it searchable and accessible through Google Podcasts.

Now, let's talk about optimizing your podcast metadata and settings to maximize visibility and discoverability. Metadata includes all the information about your podcast that you provide when uploading episodes, such as titles, descriptions, and tags. To optimize this, use keywords that your target audience is likely to search for. For example, if your podcast is about travel, include keywords like "travel tips," "adventure," and "vacation" in your descriptions and tags.

Another important aspect is your podcast's cover art. This is the first thing potential listeners see when browsing through podcasts, so make sure it's eye-catching and professional. Use high-quality images and clear, readable text. Your cover art should reflect the theme and tone of your podcast.

Lastly, pay attention to your podcast's overall settings. Make sure your release schedule is consistent, as this helps build a loyal audience. If you release episodes sporadically, listeners may lose interest. Aim for a regular schedule, whether it's weekly, bi-weekly, or monthly, and stick to it.

In this chapter, we've covered everything you need to know about publishing your podcast. From choosing a hosting platform and setting up your RSS feed to uploading episodes and optimizing your metadata, you're now equipped to share your podcast with the world. So go ahead, hit that publish button, and watch your podcast grow!

Chapter 7: Promoting Your Podcast

Welcome to Chapter 7, where we're going to talk all about promoting your podcast. You've put in the hard work creating amazing content, and now it's time to make sure people find it. Promotion is key to gaining traction and growing your audience, and this chapter will guide you through everything you need to know to develop an effective marketing strategy for your podcast.

First up, let's talk about your podcast marketing strategy. A solid strategy is essential for attracting and engaging your target audience. Think of it as your game plan for getting your podcast in front of the right people. We'll cover various tactics you can use to get the word out and make sure your episodes reach as many ears as possible.

Social media is a powerful tool for promoting your podcast. Platforms like Facebook, Twitter, Instagram, and LinkedIn can help you connect with your audience, share your episodes, and engage with listeners. Create eye-catching posts, share behind-the-scenes content, and interact with your followers to build a community around your podcast. Don't forget to use relevant hashtags to increase your visibility and reach a wider audience.

Email marketing is another effective way to promote your podcast. Building an email list allows you to communicate directly with your listeners and keep them updated on new episodes, special events, and other podcast-related news. Consider creating a newsletter where you can share exclusive content, episode highlights, and personal insights. This helps to foster a deeper connection with your audience and keeps them coming back for more.

Content promotion is also crucial. This involves sharing your podcast episodes on various platforms and repurposing your content to reach a broader audience. Write blog posts, create video snippets, and design graphics that highlight key points from your episodes. These different formats can attract people who prefer consuming content in various ways, ultimately driving more listeners to your podcast.

One of the most exciting parts of promoting your podcast is collaboration. Collaborating with other podcasters and influencers can significantly expand your reach. By appearing as a guest on other podcasts or inviting guests to yours, you can tap into their audience and introduce your podcast to new listeners. Networking with influencers in your niche can also help you gain credibility and attract a larger audience.

Building a strong network is invaluable in the podcasting world. Attend podcasting events, join online communities, and engage with other podcasters on social media. The connections you make can lead to collaborations, cross-promotions, and valuable advice from those who have been in your shoes.

In summary, Chapter 7 is all about promoting your podcast effectively to grow your audience. By developing a comprehensive marketing strategy that leverages social media, email marketing, and content promotion, you can attract and engage listeners. Additionally, collaborating with other podcasters and influencers can help you expand your reach and build a strong network. So, get ready to put these strategies into action and watch your podcast audience grow!

Chapter 8: Engaging with Your Audience

Now that your podcast is up and running, it's time to talk about one of the most important aspects of your podcasting journey: engaging with your audience. Building a loyal and engaged audience is key to the long-term success of your podcast. Without an engaged audience, your podcast is just a one-way conversation. But don't worry, I'm here to help you turn it into a vibrant community.

In this chapter, we'll dive into strategies for fostering listener engagement and feedback. I'll guide you on how to respond to listener questions, comments, and reviews to create a sense of community around your podcast. Additionally, we'll explore ways to host listener surveys, contests, and Q&A sessions to encourage active participation and interaction. So, let's get started!

Creating a Sense of Community

First things first, let's talk about creating a sense of community. Your listeners are more likely to stick around if they feel like they're part of something special. Here are a few ways to make your audience feel like they belong:

1. Acknowledge Your Listeners: Give

shout-outs to your listeners in your episodes. Mention their names, thank them for their support, and address their questions or comments. This makes them feel valued and appreciated.
2. Encourage Interaction: Prompt your listeners to interact with you. Ask them to leave comments, send in questions, or share their thoughts on social media. Make it easy for them to reach out by providing clear instructions and multiple channels of communication.
3. Be Genuine and Authentic: People connect with real, authentic voices. Be yourself, share your stories, and let your personality shine through. Your listeners will appreciate your honesty and be more likely to engage with you.

Responding to Listener Feedback

Once your audience starts engaging with you, it's crucial to respond to their feedback. This shows that you value their input and are listening to what they have to say. Here are some tips on how to handle listener feedback:

1. Respond Promptly: Try to respond to comments, questions, and reviews as quickly as possible. This shows that you're actively engaged and interested in what your listeners have to say.

2. Be Appreciative: Always thank your listeners for their feedback, whether it's positive or negative. A simple "Thank you for your input" goes a long way in building a positive relationship.
3. Address Criticism Constructively: If you receive negative feedback, don't take it personally. Instead, view it as an opportunity to improve. Address the criticism constructively, and let your listeners know that you're taking their suggestions seriously.

Hosting Listener Surveys and Contests

One great way to engage your audience is by hosting listener surveys and contests. These activities not only provide valuable insights but also make your listeners feel involved and valued. Here's how you can get started:

1. Listener Surveys: Create surveys to gather feedback on your episodes, topics, and overall podcast experience. Use tools like Google Forms or SurveyMonkey to make it easy for your listeners to participate. Share the survey link in your episodes, on social media, and in your show notes.
2. Contests: Everyone loves a good contest! Host contests where listeners

can win prizes for participating. For example, you could run a giveaway for listeners who leave reviews or share your podcast on social media. Make sure the rules are clear and the prizes are enticing.

3. Q&A Sessions: Host Q&A sessions where you answer listener questions in real-time. You can do this through live streaming on platforms like Instagram, Facebook, or YouTube. This not only encourages engagement but also gives your listeners a chance to connect with you directly.

Encouraging Active Participation

Finally, let's talk about encouraging active participation. The more engaged your audience is, the more invested they'll be in your podcast. Here are some strategies to keep your listeners actively involved:

1. Create Interactive Content: Incorporate interactive elements into your episodes, such as polls, quizzes, and challenges. This makes your content more engaging and encourages listeners to participate actively.

2. Build a Community Space: Create a dedicated space for your listeners to connect with you and each other. This

could be a Facebook group, a Discord server, or a subreddit. Foster a positive and supportive environment where listeners can share their thoughts and ideas.
3. Collaborate with Your Audience: Involve your listeners in your podcast production process. Ask for their input on episode topics, guest suggestions, or even co-hosting opportunities. This makes them feel like they're a part of your podcasting journey.

By the end of this chapter, you should have a clear understanding of how to engage with your audience and build a loyal and active community around your podcast. Remember, the key to a successful podcast is not just great content, but also a strong connection with your listeners. So, take the time to engage with your audience, listen to their feedback, and make them feel valued. Happy podcasting!

Chapter 9: Monetizing Your Podcast

Welcome to Chapter 9! This chapter is all about turning your podcasting passion into a source of income. Many podcasters have successfully found ways to monetize their shows, and we're here to help you do the same. So, let's dive into the exciting world of podcast monetization and explore the various strategies you can use.

First, let's talk about sponsorships. Sponsorships are one of the most common ways to monetize a podcast. Essentially, a company pays you to promote their products or services during your episodes. The key to successful sponsorships is finding companies that align well with your audience and niche. For example, if your podcast is about fitness, partnering with a health supplement brand or a sports equipment company could be a great fit. When you reach out to potential sponsors, be prepared to provide them with information about your audience demographics, download numbers, and engagement rates. This will help them understand the value of sponsoring your podcast.

Next up are ads. Ads can be a straightforward way to generate revenue from your podcast. There are different types of ads you can include, such as pre-roll (before the episode starts), mid-roll (in the middle of the episode), and post-roll (at the end of the episode). You can sell ad space directly to companies, or you can join a podcast advertising network that connects you with advertisers. Keep in mind that while ads can bring in money, it's important to balance them with your content to avoid overwhelming your listeners.

Another effective monetization strategy is memberships. Offering memberships can provide your most dedicated listeners with exclusive content and perks in exchange for a monthly fee. Platforms like Patreon make it easy to set up a membership program for your podcast. You can offer different tiers of membership with varying levels of benefits, such as bonus episodes, early access to new content, or behind-the-scenes insights. This not only generates revenue but also helps build a closer relationship with your loyal audience.

Identifying potential revenue streams and partnerships requires a good understanding of your audience and niche. Think about what your listeners value and what kind of products or services would genuinely interest them. You can also survey your audience to gather feedback on what they would like to see from you in terms of premium content or partnerships.

Speaking of premium content, creating additional value for your listeners can be a fantastic way to monetize your podcast. Premium content can take many forms, such as exclusive interviews, extended episodes, or specialized series on niche topics. You can offer this premium content through a subscription model or as one-time purchases. The key is to ensure that your premium content offers something unique and valuable that your regular episodes don't provide.

Let's not forget about merchandise. Selling branded merchandise like T-shirts, mugs, or stickers can be a fun and effective way to monetize your podcast while promoting your show. Many listeners love to support their favorite podcasts by purchasing and proudly displaying merchandise. Online platforms like Teespring or Printful make it easy to design and sell your own merchandise without needing to manage inventory.

Finally, consider leveraging your podcast to offer services or products related to your niche. If you have expertise in a particular area, you could offer consulting services, online courses, or workshops. Your podcast serves as a platform to showcase your knowledge and build trust with your audience, making them more likely to invest in your additional offerings.

By the end of this chapter, you'll have a solid

understanding of various monetization strategies and how to implement them. Whether it's through sponsorships, ads, memberships, premium content, merchandise, or additional services, there are plenty of ways to turn your podcasting passion into a profitable venture.

So, let's get started on the path to monetizing your podcast and turning your hard work into a rewarding source of income. Happy monetizing!

Chapter 10: Growing and Scaling Your Podcast

Congratulations! Your podcast is gaining momentum, and listeners are tuning in regularly. This is an exciting time, but it's also the perfect moment to start thinking about how you can take your show to the next level. In Chapter 10, we're going to explore how to grow and scale your podcast, ensuring its long-term success and sustainability.

First, let's talk about the importance of analyzing your podcast analytics and performance metrics. Just like a gardener checks the health of their plants, you need to keep an eye on how your podcast is doing. Most podcast hosting platforms provide a range of analytics that can give you valuable insights into your audience's behavior. You can see how many downloads each episode gets, where your listeners are located, what devices they're using, and even how long they're listening to each episode.

By regularly reviewing these metrics, you can start to identify patterns and trends. For example, you might notice that episodes on certain topics get more downloads, or that listeners tend to drop off at a specific point in your episodes. This data is incredibly valuable because it helps you understand what's working and what's not. You can then use these insights to refine your podcast strategy. If a particular topic is popular, consider creating more content around that theme. If listeners are dropping off early, maybe it's time to rethink your episode structure or pacing.

Another crucial aspect of growing your podcast is gathering and responding to listener feedback. Your audience's feedback is like a treasure trove of information. Encourage your listeners to leave reviews, send you messages, or participate in surveys. Take their comments and suggestions seriously. If multiple listeners suggest shorter episodes or more guest interviews, consider incorporating those changes. By actively engaging with your audience and making adjustments based on their feedback, you'll create a more enjoyable listening experience, which can lead to increased loyalty and word-of-mouth promotion.

Now, let's explore potential avenues for podcast expansion and diversification. One way to grow your podcast is by expanding your content offerings. This could mean branching out into new topics that are related to your original niche, or experimenting with different formats. For instance, if your podcast focuses on business tips, you might introduce a new segment where you interview successful entrepreneurs. Diversifying your content keeps your podcast fresh and interesting, and it can attract new listeners who are interested in those additional topics.

Another way to scale your podcast is by collaborating with other podcasters and influencers. Guest appearances on other podcasts can introduce your show to a new audience. Likewise, having guest hosts or co-hosts on your own podcast can bring fresh perspectives and attract their followers to your show. Networking with others in the podcasting community is a fantastic way to build relationships and grow your listener base.

Monetization is also a key factor in scaling your podcast for long-term sustainability. Once you've built a solid audience, there are several ways to monetize your podcast. You could explore sponsorships and advertising, where companies pay you to promote their products or services during your episodes. Another option is to offer premium content or bonus episodes to listeners who subscribe to a membership or Patreon. Selling merchandise related to your podcast is yet another avenue to consider. The key is to find monetization strategies that align with your brand and provide value to your listeners without compromising the quality of your content.

Lastly, maintaining the quality of your podcast is essential as you grow. As you scale, it might be tempting to cut corners or rush production, but consistency and quality are what keep listeners coming back. Consider outsourcing tasks like editing, marketing, or graphic design if it becomes too overwhelming. This allows you to focus on creating great content while ensuring all aspects of your podcast are handled professionally.

In this chapter, we've covered the essential steps to grow and scale your podcast. From analyzing analytics and incorporating listener feedback to exploring expansion opportunities and monetization strategies, you now have a roadmap to take your podcast to new heights. With "The Ultimate Guide on How to Start a Podcast," you're equipped with the knowledge and confidence to navigate your podcasting journey. So, let's dive in and uncover the endless possibilities that lie ahead in the world of podcasting!